WITHDRAWN

AVAILABLE NOW
from Lerner Publishing Services!

The *On the Hardwood* series:

Chicago Bulls
Dallas Mavericks
Los Angeles Clippers
Los Angeles Lakers
Miami HEAT
Minnesota Timberwolves
Oklahoma City Thunder
San Antonio Spurs

COMING SOON!

Additional titles in
the *On the Hardwood* series:

Boston Celtics
Brooklyn Nets
Houston Rockets
Indiana Pacers
New York Knicks
Philadelphia 76ers
Portland Trail Blazers
Utah Jazz

To Order • www.lernerbooks.com • 800-328-4929 • fax 800-332-1132

ON THE HARDWOOD

THUNDER
OKC

J.M. SKOGEN

On the Hardwood: Oklahoma City Thunder

MVP Books
2255 Calle Clara
La Jolla, CA 92037

MVP Books is an imprint of Book Buddy Digital Media, Inc., 42982 Osgood Road, Fremont, CA 94539

MVP Books publications may be purchased for
educational, business, or sales promotional use.

Cover and layout design by Jana Ramsay
Copyedited by Susan Sylvia
Photos by Getty Images

ISBN: 978-1-61570-515-3 (Library Binding)
ISBN: 978-1-61570-514-6 (Soft Cover)

TABLE OF CONTENTS

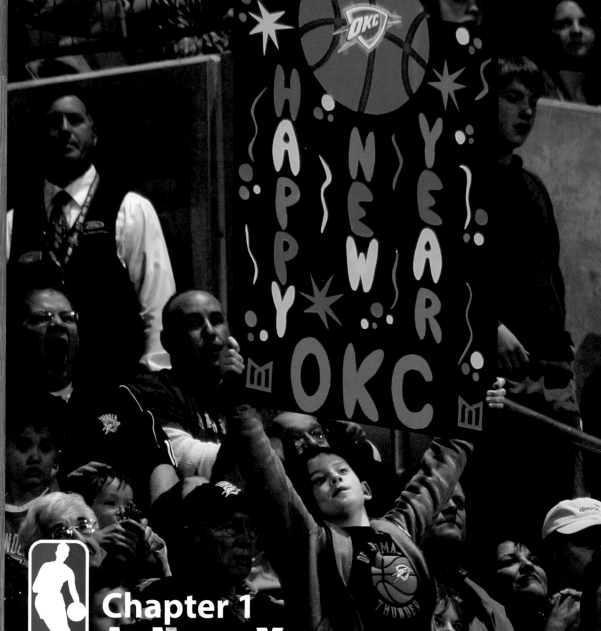

Chapter 1
A New Year

With ACDC's "Thunderstruck" blaring over the loudspeakers at Ford Center, the Oklahoma City Thunder took the court to an applause worthy of their name. Pride-filled energy pulsed through the crowd as they watched their home team—the newest team in the NBA—get ready to start the game. The new white, blue, and orange uniforms, only a few months old, now seemed so familiar. And the name, the Oklahoma City Thunder, was starting to roll off the tongue as naturally as the Boston Celtics, or the Miami Heat. Thunder fans could all agree on two things: One, they loved having a team of their very own. And two, the team was young, developing, and the city was optimistic.

Opening Night

OKC's New Year's Eve celebration is called "Opening Night," and has been around since 1987. Celebrating with the Thunder has become a new, and now unforgettable, part of this tradition.

This was not just a normal Wednesday night game. Fans flocked to the arena, cheeks still flushed from the cold December

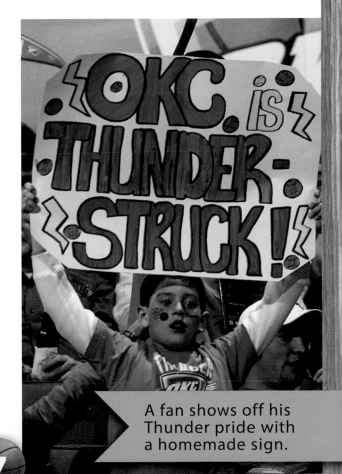

A fan shows off his Thunder pride with a homemade sign.

7

air. They were not simply there to cheer for the Thunder, but to help ring in the New Year. Oklahoma City had a tradition of throwing a city-wide party to celebrate New Year's Eve. December 31, 2008, was no exception. There were concerts, a gala, snow tubing on the local ice rink, fireworks, and even a "safari" of baby exotic animals including a kangaroo and a lemur. And this year, the city had a new addition to their holiday lineup. For the first time ever, OKC had a team that was in town to stay. Fans who went to the game were given a free pass for other events later that night all around the city. Unfortunately, many people figured they would need a little cheering up at the end of this game.

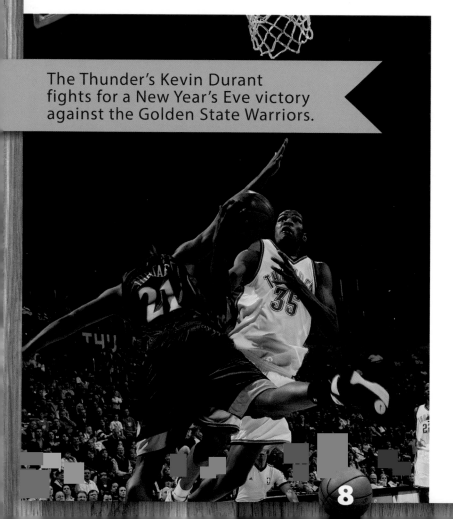

The Thunder's Kevin Durant fights for a New Year's Eve victory against the Golden State Warriors.

The Oklahoma City Thunder were playing the Golden State Warriors. The Warriors had struggled on the road that season, which should have been a good sign for Thunder fans. However, the Thunder had not had a great start to their first season. With a record of 3-29, expectations were fairly low for the home team. Royce Young, a blogger covering the Thunder, summed up these negative feelings: "More than anything, tonight is about overcoming a mental block. The Warriors aren't necessarily more talented than Oklahoma City, but OKC can't seem to shake that it's supposed to lose." Fans were happy to fill the seats at Ford Center and cheer for their team, but there wasn't much hope for a win.

However, near the end of the third quarter the crowd was

Russel Westbrook is calm and focused during the last game of 2008.

delighted, and rather surprised, to find the Thunder up by six points. If their team could just hold it together for the final quarter, they had a real shot at victory. But the fans had

In the Right Direction
After starting their first season 3-29, OKC rallied and went 20-30 to close the year.

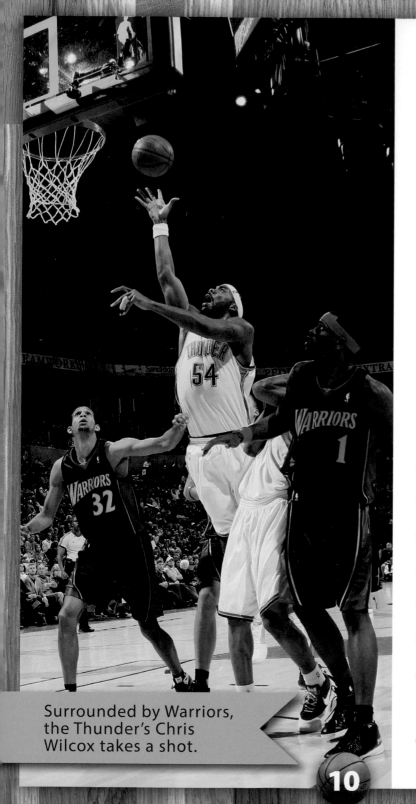

Surrounded by Warriors, the Thunder's Chris Wilcox takes a shot.

seen other games just like this earlier in the season. The Thunder would go into the fourth quarter with a lead, only to crumble under the late-game pressure. So it almost seemed natural when, just a few seconds before the third quarter buzzer, the Thunder's Chris Wilcox missed a slam dunk. The ball spun off the side of the rim, ready to be grabbed up by the Warriors. This is it, fans thought. This was the moment when the visiting team would start chipping away at the Thunder's lead, and their confidence.

But before fans could even blink, the Thunder's

Jeff Green had scooped up the ball and, in the next breath, launched himself into the air for a 15-foot jump shot. The swish of the basket, and the crowd's cheers, ended the quarter. The Thunder led 78 to 70. There was still an entire quarter to go, but at that moment, Ford Center was buzzing with hope.

But the Warriors were not done yet. By the seven-minute mark, the visitors were trailing by only three points. Fans were once again on the edge of their seats. The Thunder called a timeout, hoping to recover the focus that had carried them this far. Their coach, Scott Brooks, must have

told them to start their New Year's resolutions a day early. When they hit the court again, it was with

Jeff Green flies toward the basket.

victory in their sights. They played like a team that deserved to win, and

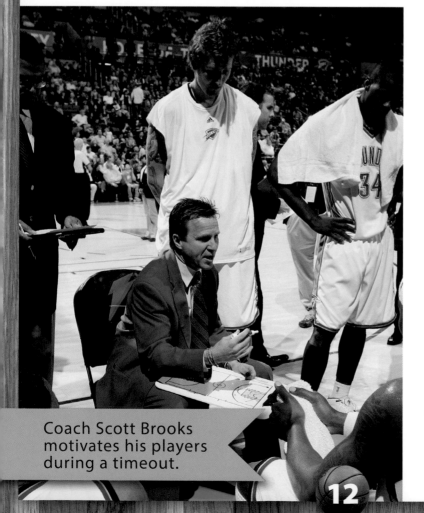

Coach Scott Brooks motivates his players during a timeout.

they trusted each other to make that happen.

In one impressive show of teamwork, Earl Watson drove towards the basket and started to jump like he was going for a layup. Then, twisting in the air, he passed the ball to Russell Westbrook, who was waiting behind him. One of the youngest players on the team, Westbrook bounced the ball once and was off. There was so much air between his shoes and the hardwood, it was like he had springs glued to his feet. After making the basket, Westbrook gave Watson a quick high five. The Warriors played well, but they just couldn't close the growing distance in the score. The Thunder scored a 107-100 victory. Midnight was still a few hours away; but for the Thunder, a new year, and a new standard of basketball, was already here.

This game proved to be a turning point for the Thunder that first season. John Rhode, a reporter for the Oklahoman, wondered, "Perhaps a light suddenly came on inside the young minds of Thunder players. Perhaps they finally got it, or they believed in themselves, or they believed in each other, or all the above." The new year brought with it a new definition of the Thunder. The young, developing team was no longer in danger of breaking the record for the worst season in NBA history. They were learning

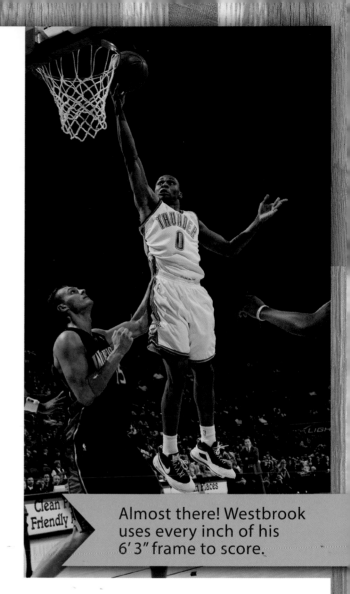

Almost there! Westbrook uses every inch of his 6′3″ frame to score.

how to win, and they played like it. And Oklahoma City was given another tradition: The Thunder has won every single New Year's Eve home game since.

WELCOME TO THUNDER BASKETBAL

Chapter 2
HELLO, THUNDER!

Several years before the Thunder became Oklahoma City's team, the city had a test run with the NBA by hosting the New Orleans Hornets. OKC had never had a basketball team before. But they had an arena, and they had a lot of basketball fans who were eager for a home team. In January of 2005, a few months before the devastation of Hurricane Katrina, Mayor Mick Cornett flew to New York City. His goal was to let NBA Commissioner David Stern know how prepared Oklahoma City was for an NBA team. David Stern responded that hockey might be a better sport for the city. But the mayor's words and enthusiasm had left a strong impression on Stern.

Then, when the New Orleans Hornets were unable to use their home arena because of the destruction caused by Hurricane

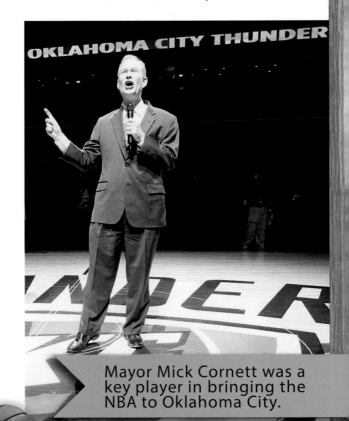

Mayor Mick Cornett was a key player in bringing the NBA to Oklahoma City.

The Hornets take on the Grizzlies at Ford Center.

Katrina, Mayor Cornett personally gave David Stern a call. He told Stern that Oklahoma City would be honored to host the team. Though many other cities wanted the Hornets to play in their arenas, Stern decided to take a chance on Oklahoma City. From 2005 to 2007, Oklahoma City embraced the Hornets as their own home team.

They packed the stands—selling out games and letting the NBA know how ready they were for a permanent team. When the Hornets returned to New Orleans, many fans wished that they didn't have to leave. But most were happy that the Hornets were finally able to go home after such a terrible natural disaster. However, they missed the excitement of the games, and the pride that came with cheering for a home team.

To attract another NBA team, the people of Oklahoma City knew they would have to make significant changes to their arena. The city had already made great advancements around the Ford Center. Downtown OKC had been transformed from a rough area of town into a lively place with new restaurants, a movie theater, and an arena that still needed a bit of work. The Ford Center had been adequate when it was built a few years earlier, but it needed to be upgraded. Things like locker rooms, scoreboards, and concession stands needed to meet NBA standards. Berry Tramel, a

Cleaning Up

Oklahoma City leaders worked hard to bring life to the heart of the city with an entertainment district, new businesses, and an NBA-worthy arena to downtown areas that used to be nearly vacant.

blogger for the Oklahoman, said that the Ford Center was "built on the cheap," and that the fans saw it as "functional, nothing more." But Oklahoma City didn't want to settle for "functional." They wanted an arena that would reflect their enthusiasm and their desire to have a permanent basketball team.

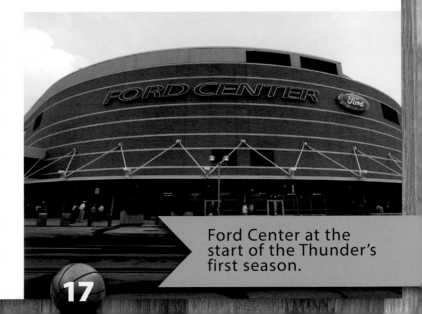

Ford Center at the start of the Thunder's first season.

Renamed in 2011 to Chesapeake Energy Arena, the Thunder's home was new and improved for the 2011-12 season.

So the city took action, voting on a plan to improve Ford Center. Just a few of the changes would include a bigger entrance, new team locker rooms, rooftop gardens, and better suites. It would take years for all of the improvements to be made. But with this step, Oklahoma City declared itself to be a future home of the NBA. And, luckily for OKC, the NBA took notice. When owner Clay Bennett decided to move his team to another city, Oklahoma City had already showed that it was a community of eager fans, ready to embrace another team. They just wanted a team that would stay for more than a few seasons.

With the team beginning play in 2008, Oklahoma City had a lot of work to do. Before they could design uniforms, or plan the advertising, they needed to choose one simple, yet very important thing—a name.

Clay Bennett wanted a name that not only reflected the strength of his players, but one that captured the spirit of their new home.

On September 3, 2008, at the team's headquarters in downtown Oklahoma City, Bennett climbed a podium. He was ready to announce the official name. Until this moment, all of the team's practice uniforms had simply read "OKC-NBA." The team was ready for a real identity, and in just a few minutes, everyone would hear the name, and see the official logo and colors.

There were hundreds of people gathered around, waiting to hear Bennett say

The OKC Twisters?
Some of the other Oklahoma City team names that were considered were the Barons, Twisters, and Renegades.

a name they already knew. A few weeks before this announcement, the name had been leaked, and even certain items were already listed on the NBA's online store. It wasn't just curiosity that drove all these people

OKC Thunder owner Clay Bennett addresses a crowd during the naming ceremony.

19

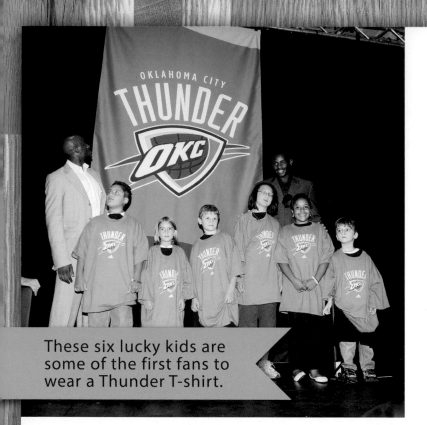

These six lucky kids are some of the first fans to wear a Thunder T-shirt.

The OKC Thunder's logo was unveiled to ACDC's "Thunderstruck"—a song that would become a kind of anthem for the team. A plain, black banner hung beside the podium, and it simply read, "Oklahoma City." Then, as the song began, the word "Thunder" being chanted over and over, the banner dropped away. A bright blue banner was revealed, with the words "Oklahoma City Thunder," and the now-famous yellow, blue and orange-red logo beneath. Beside the banner, six children put on new blue T-shirts, all proudly displaying the team's logo.

Bennett had many reasons for choosing this name, and the colors

to come and listen—though they did want to make sure the rumored name was correct. They stood before that podium wanting to be a part of their team's history from the very first moment.

Local Color

The orange-red in the Thunder's team colors is also meant to be a mix of the local college team colors. The University of Oklahoma uses a crimson red, while Oklahoma State uses orange.

of the logo. The colors included the blue of the state flag, the yellow of the sun, and the reddish-orange of the sunset. The name "Thunder" was chosen to remind fans of Oklahoma's famous storms, and also their local history. The Army's 45th Infantry Division, based in Oklahoma City, were called the "Thunderbirds." A Thunderbird was a legend from Native American lore, whose wings could cause the wind to howl, and thunder to rumble.

This was exactly what Oklahoma City wanted—a team that would cause storms to rage, and make the earth tremble. And most importantly, they wanted a team that was entirely their own. When the season started a month later, Oklahoma City crowded into Ford Center to see the new uniforms, and chant their team's name. They were ready to be fans again.

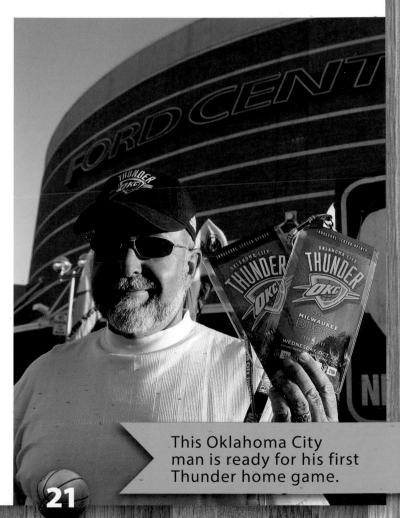

This Oklahoma City man is ready for his first Thunder home game.

Chapter 3
NEXT YEAR STARTS NOW

Ford Center was full of bright blue shirts and a sense of wonder. Fans watched the Thunder battle the Lakers in the first round of the 2010 playoffs, another tangible step in the team's development. The Thunder had forced this series to Game 6. But the Lakers only needed to win tonight's game to move on to the next round. Looking back to just the previous season, when the Thunder had been in danger of breaking the record for the worst single-season record ever, this was an amazing accomplishment.

At the start of the 2009-10 season, there was every hope for an improvement over the last year's 23-59 losing record. In fact, when ESPN had predicted how each team would do in the coming season,

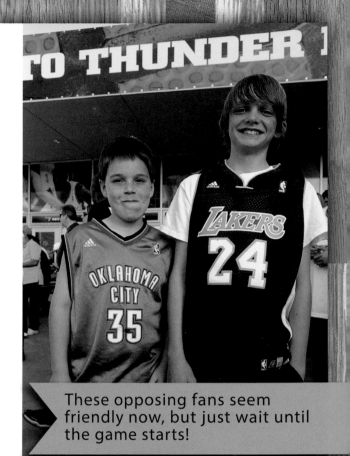

These opposing fans seem friendly now, but just wait until the game starts!

they had forecasted 32 wins and 50 losses for the Thunder. But no one besides Oklahoma City had thought that the Thunder would reverse that

Youth VS. History
2009-10 was the Thunder's first post-season appearance, but the Lakers were familiar with the playoffs—they had only missed the playoffs five times since the franchise started in 1948.

prediction, winning 50 games and losing only 32.

ESPN had also written about the buzz that surrounded the young Thunder, with such players as Kevin Durant and Russell Westbrook already showing great promise: "It's not hard to see what the excitement is about. But it will be hard to see them on TV." The Thunder only had three nationally televised games in the regular season. But all 82 regular season games were broadcast on local channels to a huge number of fans—those who weren't packing the arena in person. And on this particular night, the Thunder were *definitely* on national TV.

The Thunder have also become a very familiar sight to the people of OKC. Thunder players have made over 900 visits to community

Kevin Durant dribbles around the Lakers' Ron Artest on his way to the basket.

groups. Players rebuild homes in the city, lead clinics on obesity prevention, read to children, and distribute free books—a lot of them. Via the Rolling Thunder Book Bus, the team has distributed 57,000 books to students throughout OKC. In addition to free books, the Thunder players also treat their young fans to free tickets. The Tickets for Kids program offers kids a chance to see their favorite team in person. The Thunder represent more than wins and losses. The team also stands for their fans, and the organization takes sincere pride in positively impacting the community every day of the year, not just on game

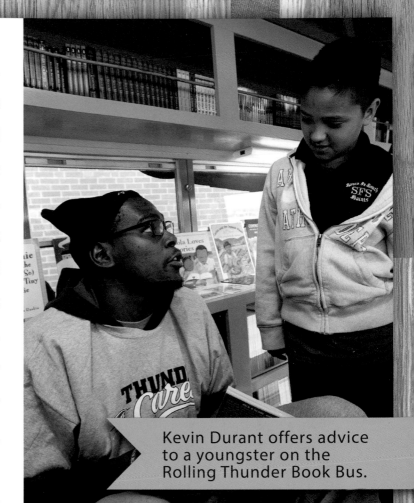

Kevin Durant offers advice to a youngster on the Rolling Thunder Book Bus.

days. For all of these reasons, *ESPN the Magazine* recently ranked the Thunder as the number one professional sports franchise for fan relations. There is no question that the Thunder have become a vital part of OKC's community.

A True Survivor

A large American elm tree, called the Survivor Tree, resides at the Oklahoma City National Memorial. It was nearly killed by the blast, but it eventually bloomed again, and is now thriving.

The Thunder players wanted to embrace their new city just as much as the city wanted them. Even before the first season started, the players all took a trip to the Oklahoma City National Memorial. This memorial was built to honor the victims of the terrible bombing on April 19, 1995, which killed 168 people. This was the worst terrorist attack in the United States until September 11,

The Oklahoma City National Memorial has one empty chair for every victim of the attack.

2001. Before the Thunder took the local spotlight with their unlikely winning season, that attack was what many people in the country thought of first, when they thought of Oklahoma City. The bombing is still one of the top Google search results for "Oklahoma", just after the Thunder, and the musical *Oklahoma!* The team wanted to understand Oklahoma City's past, before they become a huge part of their future. And they wanted to show their respect for what this great city had overcome. It has since become a tradition for all new players to visit the memorial before they even start their first practice.

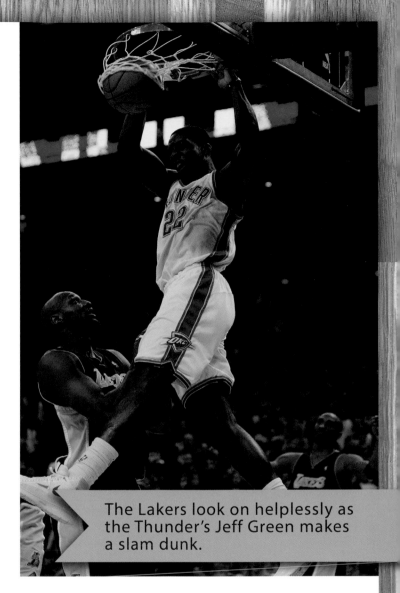

The Lakers look on helplessly as the Thunder's Jeff Green makes a slam dunk.

Tonight's game was just over a week after the 15th anniversary of that horrible bombing. The people of Oklahoma City were making some serious noise, and earning

Ford Center's nickname of Loud City. This had been a hard-fought game. The Lakers were ahead for most of the game, but with one second left in the fourth quarter, the Thunder found themselves leading by one point, 94-93. The Lakers' Kobe Bryant had the ball and was forcing his way up the side of the key. The Thunder's point guard Russell Westbrook was defending him like a second shadow, planting himself right on Bryant's hip. But he couldn't stop Bryant from taking a wild fadeaway shot. Bryant threw himself back, away from Westbrook, sending the

Thunder fans watch as Kobe Bryant takes a shot against defender Russell Westbrook.

ball right towards the basket. The entire arena gasped as it bounced off the rim.

For an instant, the crowd thought the Thunder had defeated the mighty Lakers. They could picture the ball falling to the ground, and hear the buzzer signalling victory for their team. But the ball was snatched out of the air by the Lakers' seven-foot-tall forward center, Pau Gasol. When Gasol slammed that ball into the net, it was all but over. With half a second left on the clock, the Thunder attempted a last, desperate shot. They passed Westbrook the ball, and he fired a lightning fast 23-foot jump shot from the very edge of the arc—and missed.

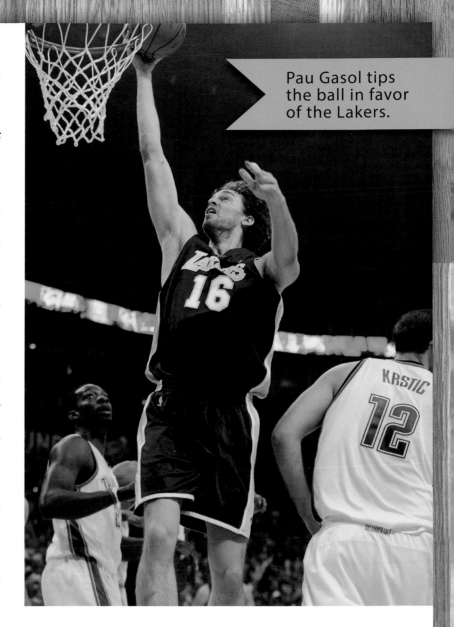

Pau Gasol tips the ball in favor of the Lakers.

The players were devastated. Jeff Green bent over, holding his head in his hands. Kevin Durant fell to the floor and slammed his hands to the ground in disappointment. But the crowd—right after the buzzer marked the end of their team's second season, got to their feet and cheered. They stood there, clapping and shouting and beating their thunder sticks as loud as they could. The Oklahoma City Thunder might have lost this game, but their city cheered for them anyway. They

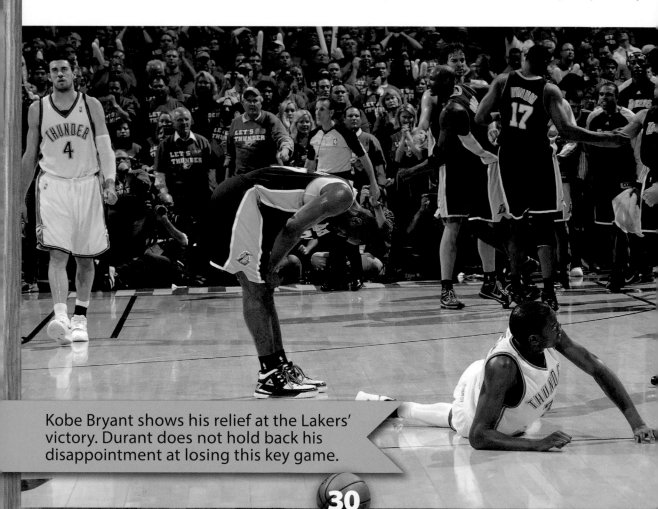

Kobe Bryant shows his relief at the Lakers' victory. Durant does not hold back his disappointment at losing this key game.

stood while the two teams lined up and shook hands. And they kept standing, clapping, and roaring for their team for about 10 minutes. Because, when it all came down to it, this wasn't just their team anymore. The Thunder were a part of their city—a part of themselves. And they were so proud.

In the moments after this first round loss, Kevin Durant spoke to his team about how far they had come, and how far they would go. Durant told them, "Next year starts now." This comment must have sounded very familiar to the people of Oklahoma City. For the Thunder,

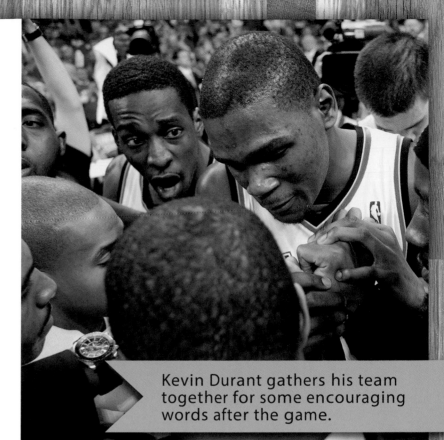

Kevin Durant gathers his team together for some encouraging words after the game.

and the entire city, a loss didn't mean the end of the world. With their strength and determination, it was only the beginning.

A Picture of Strength

Oklahoma City's mayor had a photo of Durant and Green leaning on each other after losing this game against the Lakers. To him, it represented the city's ability to overcome loss and make itself better.

The NBA blends the best athletes from all over the globe on 30 teams. The Thunder are a prime example of people with different backgrounds working together for a common goal. There was the slender shooter from Washington, D.C., and the lightning-quick point guard from Los Angeles who wasn't supposed to reach the NBA. There was the 6'10" shot-swatter from the Republic of Congo, and his bearded friend from Los Angeles. Four players, four different stories, and one goal in mind: an NBA Championship.

Kevin Durant was always a basketball player. Raised with the help of his

grandmother as one of four children in Washington, D.C., Durant spent his early years shaping his game alongside other current NBA players, like Michael Beasley, Ty Lawson, and

In 2007, while at the University of Texas, Durant was named NABC Division I Player of the Year.

Greivis Vasquez. Even among his peers, Durant stood out. In 2007, Durant and Greg Oden were not only two of the best college players in the nation, they were competing to be the number one pick in the 2007 NBA Draft. Oden eventually was selected before Durant so KD (Durant's initials and his nickname) would set out to Seattle to begin his career.

Durant did not start slowly. He was Rookie of the Year in 2008, and even more accomplishments, both personally and for his team, started rolling in from there. NBA All-Star? Check. NBA scoring champion? Check. All-NBA First Team? Check. NBA All-Star Game MVP? Check. Western Conference champion? Check. Olympic gold medalist?

Wearing their 2012 Olympic Gold, Kevin Durant and Russell Westbrook, along with the Heat's LeBron James, stand for the National Anthem.

Check. While Durant was always known as a "can't miss" kid for his sweet jump shot and the high odds that he would reach the NBA, his buddy from Los Angeles was less of a sure thing.

Russell Westbrook was 5'8" and a slim 140 pounds when he entered high school. He didn't even start for his varsity team until his junior year. Then, Westbrook started growing—and he didn't stop. When his senior year began, Westbrook had shot up to 6'3". But College offers were still not overwhelming. Westbrook enjoyed a bit of good fortune, though, when UCLA's point guard Jordan Farmar declared for the NBA Draft. All of a sudden,

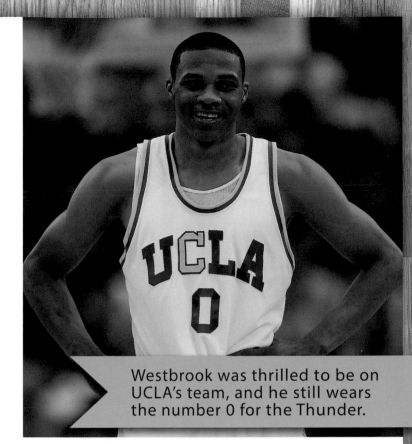

Westbrook was thrilled to be on UCLA's team, and he still wears the number 0 for the Thunder.

UCLA needed a point guard, and they extended a scholarship offer to Westbrook. From there, Westbrook took care of the rest, eventually

In Remembrance

A childhood friend of Westbrook's, Khelcey Barrs, collapsed and died on the basketball court in 2004. Westbrook wears KB3, Barrs' initials and number, on a wristband to this day.

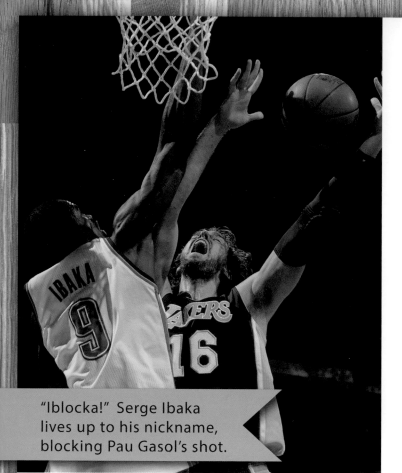

"Iblocka!" Serge Ibaka lives up to his nickname, blocking Pau Gasol's shot.

soon became known for his basketball skills and for his shot-blocking ability. His nickname, 'Iblocka' instead of Ibaka, reflects the fact that he led the NBA in blocked shots in the 2011-12 season. At 6'10", Ibaka is a rim protector defensively. His offensive game is developing nicely as well, which was evident when Ibaka was a perfect 11-11 against San Antonio in Game 4 of the 2012 Western Conference Finals.

joining Durant as an NBA All-Star and Olympic gold medalist.

L.A. is a long way from the Congo, so if Westbrook wasn't well-known, Serge Ibaka was even less so. Ibaka first had to distinguish himself in his own family, as he was one of 18 children. Ibaka

As far as scoring, James Harden was instant offense. The NBA's Sixth Man of the Year in 2012, Harden was brought off the bench with the intent to score and create opportunities for the Thunder.

Beyond Harden's sweet jump shot, he has created quite a following with a beard that he's had since 2009. Too lazy to shave in college, Harden started growing a beard—which now has its own Twitter account and Facebook page. 'Fear the Beard' has become a popular saying in OKC. But even if opponents

don't fear the beard, they must at least respect Harden and his three buddies, as they are the building blocks for an organization on the rise.

It is easy to recognize James Harden fans... just look for the beards!

As the 2011-12 season opened, the Oklahoma City Thunder had only been in existence for four short years—a young team with young players. The "oldest" team in the NBA in 2012 was the Dallas Mavericks, with an average age of 30.33. The Thunder, on the other hand, were one of the five youngest teams, with an average age of 25.46 years old.

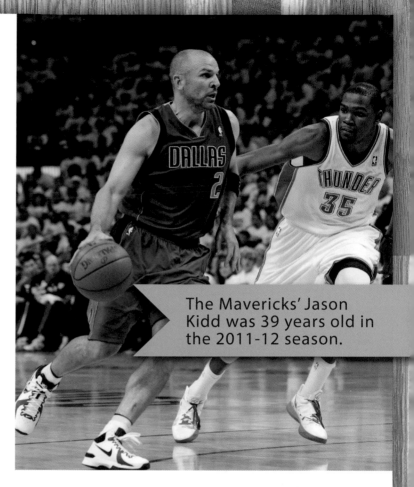

The Mavericks' Jason Kidd was 39 years old in the 2011-12 season.

Up until the 2012 Western Conference Playoffs, many critics thought the Thunder had a lot of potential. But they weren't convinced that the Thunder had the experience to be real contenders. For the past 13 years, only three teams had won the Western Conference Finals: the Los Angeles Lakers, the San Antonio Spurs, and the Dallas Mavericks. Could the Thunder really break that 13-year streak and go on

Get Well Soon!

Durant dedicated his 2011-12 season to former teammate Jeff Green. Green was traded to the Celtics in 2011, but was unable to play due to a heart condition that needed surgery.

to the NBA Finals? Oklahoma City fans cheered "Yes!" But much of the country thought that the Finals were still a few years away for this growing franchise.

But then the Thunder swept the Dallas Mavericks in the first round of the playoffs, knocking last year's NBA Champions out of the running. The rumblings began that maybe, just maybe, this young team might have a chance after all. Then they beat the Lakers in the next round, and even crushed them by 29 points in the first game of the series. In two rounds, the Thunder had not only beaten the last two Western Conference Champions, but the last two NBA Champions. Now they would come face to face with the San Antonio Spurs.

Going into the Western Conference Finals, the Spurs had an 18-game winning streak. They also had been NBA champions four of the last 13 years. Many people

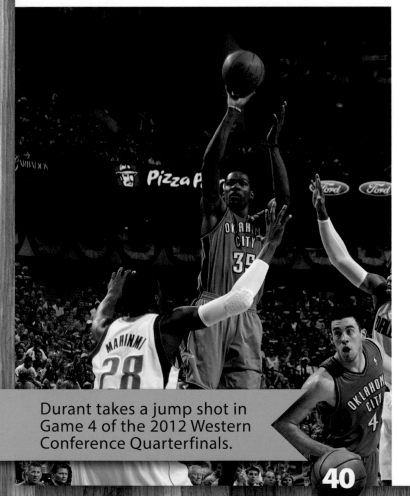

Durant takes a jump shot in Game 4 of the 2012 Western Conference Quarterfinals.

thought that the Thunder had had a great run, but there was little chance that they would actually win the series. The first two games began to prove those doubters right. The Spurs took the first two games in San Antonio. It looked like this might be a very quick series.

After those first two losses, the Thunder's coach, Scott Brooks, had the team sit down and watch video of their losing efforts. He wanted his team to watch their play, and figure out how they could improve. Brooks also wanted his players to point out the Spurs' weaknesses to prove that they were indeed beatable. They weren't about

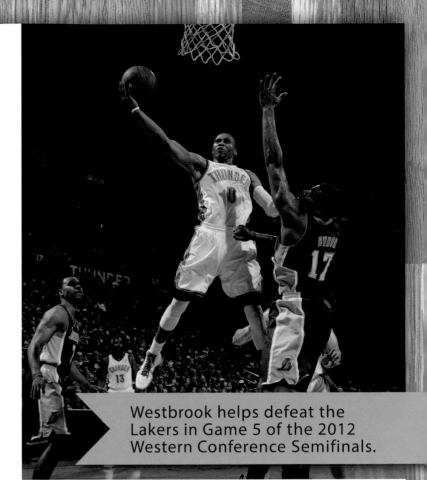

Westbrook helps defeat the Lakers in Game 5 of the 2012 Western Conference Semifinals.

to risk a three-game-to-zero hole without first doing their homework.

At the beginning of Game 3, the Thunder and the crowd seemed to

Spurred to Success

Beyond winning 18 games in a row, the Spurs have another streak to their name. They've been to the playoffs every year since 1998, and have only missed the playoffs four times.

The Thunder's James Harden goes up against the Spurs' Tiago Splitter in Game 3

feed off the each other's energy. The Thunder scored the game's first eight points. For the fans who had come to watch the second Western Conference Finals in OKC, this was exactly the kind of game that they wanted. The Thunder were in complete control. During a breathtaking play in the first quarter, Westbrook caught the rebound when the Spurs missed a shot. Westbrook passed it to Durant. Durant slowly dribbled up the court, until he came to one of the Spurs' defenders at the top of the key. Then Durant seemed to flip a switch, and was suddenly accelerating. He

Mascot of the Year

Rumble the Bison makes over 400 appearances in the community every year. His home-game performances and community service made quite an impression on the NBA. He was named Mascot of the Year in 2009, his very first year as the Thunder's mascot.

drove the ball around the defender and up the side of the key. Then, with his feet never touching the paint, Durant flew through the air to the basket. He slammed the ball through the net, and the crowd exploded in amazement.

But the Spurs were not going to let the Thunder take this game without a fight. After making two free throws at the end of the first quarter, the Spurs were leading by two points. Could this be the beginning of the end for the Thunder in this series? The Thunder quickly gave the world their answer: absolutely not!

In the first two minutes of the

The Oklahoma City Thunder mascot, Rumble the Bison, gets the crowd amped up.

The Thunder's Russell Westbrook and Serge Ibaka step in to cut off Gary Neal's lane to the basket.

second quarter, the ball never seemed to leave the Thunder's hands. They put nine points on the board, firmly wrenching the lead away from the Spurs. And they never gave it back. For the entire second half of the game, the Thunder led by at least 10 points. The margin ultimately climbed to 20, with a final score of 102-82. The Thunder didn't just break the Spurs' winning streak, they shattered it all over the court.

When asked how the Thunder were able to make such a complete turnaround, Coach Scott Brooks responded: "We just played a good basketball game. We played with a lot of force, we played with good energy, but we played defensive-minded basketball. That's who we are. That's how we win." This wasn't just some mistake. The Thunder had learned how to take on the Spurs, and they would use that knowledge to beat the Spurs in the next three games. Now, for the first time, the Thunder were Western Conference Champions. They were going to the Finals.

Almost There!
For the past three years, the only teams to beat the Thunder in the playoffs were teams who went on to win the NBA Championship.

The Thunder won the first game of the Finals on their home court against the Miami Heat. Unfortunately, this was the last game that they would win in the 2011-12 postseason. The Heat took the next four games, sending the Thunder

The Spurs' defenders can't stop Kevin Durant as he soars to the basket.

Grace through the Loss

During the Thunder's last timeout of Game 5, Coach Scott Brooks told his team to hold their heads up high and congratulate the Heat like champions, because they deserved the victory this year.

back home to Oklahoma City without a trophy. But when the players arrived back in Oklahoma City, they were met by thousands of fans who had gathered at the airport to greet them. This wasn't really a planned celebration, but still over 4,000 people came to show their love and support for their team. The Thunder players took turns addressing their fans, telling them that next year they would bring home the NBA Championship. But, for the thousands of beaming faces in the crowd, they knew that they had already won. This amazing, athletic, beloved team was here to stay.

Oklahoma City is always ready to come out and support its team.

Kevin Durant holds up the 2012 Western Conference Championship trophy.